GREEK PLACES

Mount Athos

Rekos

SERIES: GREEK PLACES/12

Written by: Theocharis Provatakis
Photographs by: Th. Provatakis-N. Kontos-I. Rekos
Translation by: Christine Machera

ISBN 960-7167-29-5

© Copyright
Ⓟ I. REKOS Ltd 13, Ag. Mina str., tel. 031 - 696 587, 696 070, Thessaloniki

◄

God the Father with the Twenty - four Elders: wall - painting in Xiropotamou Monastery (1783).

Agion Oros (The Holy Mountain)

Athos is one of the most important places, not only of Greece and the Emos peninsula, but of the whole world because of its great national, historical, theological, philosophical, Christian and artistic value. Aghion Oros, a pole of the Orthodox monastic life, as well as of the arts and culture, was for centuries a tower of light and a point of reference for the orthodox people.

During the period of the Turkish rule, it was a shelter for the Greek culture and education and the center of the reanimation of the Greek Nationalism and Greek Education. Aghion Oros, besides having an intellectual content, has an architecture which is like music composed by the Almighty made accesible to all people's hearts.

HISTORICAL INSIGHTS

During the pre-Christian years and until the beginning of the Third Century B.C., there were several towns in Athos such as Sani, Thisson, Klinai, Dion and others which are mentioned by Thoucydides, Ploutarchos, Homer, Apollonios and by other ancient authors. These towns began disappearing during the third century without anyone ever knowing what happened to them. According to Ploutarchos, the Stassikrates (or according to Stravona, Dinokrates), proposed to Alexander the Great (336-332 B.C.) who was contemplating on building a town to remind people of his glory, to convert the mountain of Athos into a statue of himself, so people would see the grandeur of Macedonia. The statue would represent Alexander «holding up in his left hand a town of 10.000 people and in his right hand a river leading into the sea».

Alexander the Great, though didn't agree with this plan, and replied to Dinokrates telling him to «Leave Aghion Oros as it is». It was enough that another king made a fool of himself forever, after, digging through the mountain's meaning the digging which Xerxi's engineer Vounares attempted in 481 B.C., when they marched against the Greeks with a fleet of 1.200 large ships.

The first Christian came to the Athos peninsula during the years of Great Constantine. It is assumed from various sources that during the years of Julian the Apostate (361-363 B.C.) there were not only Christians

A Monk while working on his artistic offering.

Animate and inanimate praise God. Fresco 1739.

living there, but idolaters as well.

From the third century until the ninth century, the whole area was destroyed by barbarian invaders. The invaders destroyed all the written documents so everything we know is totally based on the legends and traditions through the years.

According to several written documents the monks appeared officially in the 9th century. At the beginning they settled in, near the Isthmus and later on moved and occupied the most distant and remote, ragged areas of Aghion Oros.

Even during an earlier stage, that is in 842, a delegation from Aghion Oros participated at the Synod of Constantinople. During the middle of the 9th century the figures of Paul the Xeropotamite and Athanassios the Athonian appeared. The two monks built monasteries and they gathered the other monks there. Little by little, impressive buildings, as well as large temples and guest-houses were built. At the same time many young people joined the monks.

THE MONASTIC FOUNDATIONS OF ATHOS

Aghion Oros, comprises today monastic foundations which can be divided into six (6) categories; abbeys, skites, cells, huts, seats and hermitages. The number of the abbeys -which cannot be increased or decreased- is twenty. Seventeen of them are Greek (Megistes Lavras, Vatopediou, Iviron, Dionysiou, Koutloumoussiou, Pantokratoros, Xerepotamou, Dohiariou, Katakalou, Phitotheou, Simonos Petras, Aghiou Pavlou, Stavronikita, Xenofontos, Grigoriou, Esfigmenou, Constamonitou), one is Russian, (Saint Panteleimona), one is Serbian (Helandariou) and one is Bulgarian (Zographou). The number of the other monastic foundations is subject to changes.

Festival at the Monastery of Saint Panteleimona.

Until, just before the last war broke out the inhabitants of Aghion Oros, men only, according to an old and inviolable rule, were 5.431, 5.000 of whom were monks. Today the monks are about 1.600. Usually the abbeys are surrounded by four-story and quadrilateral buildings where the monks' cells are placed into different sections. Externally the buildings have balconies which are called aplotaries .

In the peculiar abbeys, the monks occupy more than one room forming small apartments which all have celars. In the cenobitics each monk has a small rectangular room with very few things in it. Each abbey acts as a separate patriarchical vasilica.

All the monks acquire the Greek citizenship when they become novices or when they become monks, without any further proceedures in Mount

Left: Vatopediou Monastery. Above: Xenofondos Monastery.
Below: Pages from a liturgical text; bombycine codex in Vatopediou Monastery.

Above right: A monk returning from work; below: Evening on Mount Athos.

Monastery of Saint Panteleimona. Monks in an old picture.

Athos. Besides the twenty abbeys, there are also fourteen skites, huts, seats and hermitages.

At Karies –the capital of Aghion Oros–, an Ecclesiastical School operates for the novices and monks who wish to be educated. Today the population of Aghion Oros consists of Greek, Russian, Serbian, Bulgarian and Rumanian monks.

All the abbeys and the cenobitic skites have the image of a small fortified city. Each abbey is surrounded by a strong wall which in the earlier days was fairly competent enough to provide safe residency. On the walls there are towers with battlement loopholes which made fighting with the pirates more effective. Most of the temples have wall paintings and they are rebuilt in a special architectural form which is called Aghioritikos .

Cenobitics and Peculiar Abbeys

The abbeys are distinguished in cenobitics and peculiar abbeys. In the cenobitics everything is common. Roof, work, food and prayer. The legislative authority is conducted by the senate which comprises eminent monks. The administrative authority is

▶

Jesus Christ and the Samaritan. Modern portable icon.

conducted by the abbot who is the lifelong master and the spiritual father of the abbey. He is elected by the monks who are in the abbey's service for at least six years. In the peculiar abbeys, which are seven, everything is common, beside food. A committee appoints the work that has to be done and each monk carries out his duty for which he gets a meager salary.

The legislative authority is conducted by the gathering of the supervisors. Its members are elected for life by the gathering. The administrative authority is conducted by a committee which has two or three members who are selected from the supervisors for a period of one year.

Riding around Athos.

The Skites

The Skites are groups of monks' houses which have been founded in an abbey's area. The founding is done by an Abbey's Act and is ratified by a decree from the Patriarchate. The number of the monks has been defined by the Act of Founding. The regulation of the interior operations of the Skite is approved by the abbey. The skites are peculiars or cenobitics. The peculiars are a gathering of huts around a main temple which is called «Kyriaco». Each cell has its own very small temple. Anyway, all the monks on Sundays and holidays, have their divine services in the Kyriako , while during the rest of the days they have their

Festival prearation.

services in their cells.

The head of a skite is called Diakos and he is elected by the older monks of the cells for a period of one year. He takes care of matters such as caring for the hospitality of the pilgrims as well as for the performance of the divine services in the Kyriako . He also represents the skite wherever it's needed. At the cenobitic skites the Dikaios who is called Abbot, heads and leads the skite until his death

Momentum from the millenium celebration (1963).

and his election is approved by the abbey. Their buildings are like those of the abbeys but they can never become abbeys. Today there are 14 cells in total.

The Cells

The Cells of Aghion Oros are foundations with one temple and a building which consists of cells and auxiliary rooms. Head of the cell is the Old-Man and the rest are his attendants. The number of the monks cannot be more than nine. They support themselves, by cultivating a small piece of land, painting and sculpturing the wood to form icons, making mortars and worry-beads .

The Huts

The huts are small and isolated residences for two or three monks which have been granted to them for life by the abbey to which the territory belongs. The monks in the huts support themselves with their handi-work.

The Seats

The seats are small huts with only one monk. The abbey grants the seat to the monk. He lives for life there and he takes from the abbey only the absolutely essential food which is called coumbana.

The Hermitages

The hermitages are small seats. They are at deserted and sacred places, sometimes on rocks and inaccessible summits and sometimes in caves and clefts of rocks where the monks establish their inaccessible refuges. They live there on fasts, wakefulness and endless prayers, studying the Testaments and the phenomenon of death. All the establishments at Athos operate according to the Byzantine twenty-four hour system and according to the Julian calendar. When the sun sets, the time in Athos is 12.00 during all seasons with the exception of the Iveron abbey where the time is 12.00 when the sun rises.

Treasures and gems

There are many gems, treasures and manuscripts which Aghion Oros has in its possession and is proud about. Despite many plunders and destructions which this land has suffered, a good number of treasures were preserved. Gems, unique in the world, are being kept today safely and are exhibited only in special occasions and with proper devoutness. These precious treasures, for many years were a tempting target for the invaders, because Aghion Oros didn't maintain a local defense army system (neither during the Byzantine period, nor during the Turkish rule). As a result of the constant invasions, the monks were required to be on the alert for invaders, keeping the gems in boxes and sacs, so they could hide them in special hiding places in the towers or in the basements with the help of the serdarides and the seimenides (a branch of the gendarmes). We should mention the relics of saints the reliquaries, the crosses which are made of wood from the Holy-Cross, the Epitaphs and icons, the gospels, the sacerdotal vestments, the mosaics, the chalices, the sceptres, items of rare artistic value and cases which hold crosses.

These items are only a fraction of the treasures of Aghion Oros. Many of these treasures are precious, not only from an artistic but also from a historical point of view. A good number of old rare documents with a great historical and artistic value are being kept in the archives of the abbeys.

These documents, not only reveal the various historical stages but also connect this land

Warrior saints: wall - painting in the main church of Vatopediou Monastery.

The clock with the "Negro" ornament on the facade of Vatopediou Monastery's main church.

The well with its splendid cover at Vatopediou.

The harmony of buildings and a calm sea.

"Praise Him, young men and maidens...": wall - painting in the Great Laura.

with events and acts of great importance. Furthermore, some items of great value at the abbey of Agia Lavra are the following: the sac with the crown of emperor Nikiforos Fokas, a piece from the Holy-Cross, a gospel decorated with pearls, two heavy gospels, the cross and the sceptre of the founder Athanassios the Athonite, sacerdotal vestments and several other antiques and gems.

Furthermore, all the abbeys of Athos have their own precious private collections of antiques and gems, kings' presents and many other items like the Virgin's Belt and small pictures of Empress Theodora which are called ninia .

The largest piece known worldwide of the Holy-Cross is kept at the abbey of Vatopedi, while at the abbey of Xeropotamou one can find the cup which belonged to the Empress Poulheria and which is called Pantzechri , along with other precious items such as sacerdotal vestments, pieces of the reed and the sponge which was given to Jesus. The largest bell in Athos and the second largest in the whole world is found at the abbey of St. Panteleimona, and weighs 15.000 kgs. In addition one can find icons and other valuable treasures which are unique.

The libraries at the abbeys are full of manuscripts containing codes which exceed 12.500.

Dafne (Laurel)

Dafne is the port of Aghion Oros. It's name comes from the large number of laurels (dafne in Greek) which grow there. The «Serdaris», the policemen and the customs officeres await the visitors at the pier. The Serdaris dressed in his uniform, the customary foustanella and red cap, is willing to give any kind of information to the visitors, or to show them the way to their destination. Life's pace here is rather slow. Monks and visitors mingle together, but don't pay much attention to each other. The monks are interested in their religious and intellectual duties, while the visitors are trying to explore this holy-land.

From Dafne to Karies

The distance from Dafne to Karies is 12 kilometers. On your way to Karies (which is higher than Dafne), you can see ravines full of trees, plantations and mountains all around the snow-covered summit of Mount Athos. Going on foot is a very enjoyable experience. It's like exploring a dreamland. You are going constantly from one forrest to another and from one summit to another. The sun is hardly visible and one is protected by its rays walking under the deep while one can admire the various types of wildflowers and blossoms. As soon as you pass the Xeropotamou abbey, down at the opposite slope you can see three

Fresco from the Protato.

cells. As they say, it's in one of those cells where Kazantzakis became acquainted with monasticism and later on became famous.

As soon as you reach the top you can see at your right hand the meadow of Xeropotamos which has many filbert-trees, apple-trees and chest-nut trees and is surrounded by thousands of acres of forrests. You can see hills and valleys, mountains and ravines, chestnut-trees and very tall cypresses. All these, along with the background of the snow-covered mountain of Athos, form an unforgettable view. The rolling hills are covered with cypresses, plane-trees, fir-trees and several other kind of trees. From time to

Dafni.

The wonder - working icon "Dignum Es

Aerial view of Karies.

time you can see cells, surrounded by trees. All around there are hundreds of acres of chestnuts which are the natural wealth of Mount Athos. Its huge trunks follow one another like there's been some kind of mysterious pact between them. In many places the trunks are covered by large ivies giving the impression of forming an endless roof.

Karies

Karies is the capital of Aghion Oros. One thousand years ago it was called Messi and now has a few dozen houses and a few temples. At the beginning of the 11th century it was called Lavra of Karies, while at the end of the 14th century (1394) it was called Skite of Karies.

The building of the «sacred community» where the representatives from the abbeys meet, is at the center of this little town. In front of this building stands the temple of Protato. All around there are several small shops. Nineteen larger houses in several spots, which are called konakia, are the residences of the representatives. Only the Koutloumoussiou abbey doesn't have such a house because of its proximity to Karies. Furthermore, there are eighty-two cells in and around Karies, with monks from Greece, Russia, Roumania, Bulgaria, and

Yugoslavia which belong to various abbeys.

A necessary requirement for a visit to Aghion Oros is the DIAMONITIRIO (Permit to Reside) which is issued by the highest officials of Aghion Oros, i.e., the «Sacred Community» after they receive a note from the Police Station of Karies. It is signed by the Head-supervisor and the other supervisors of the holy-land and it's sealed with the small or the large seal of the «Sacred Community», depending always on who the visitor making the request is, or who is recommending a potential visitor.

The Protato

The Protato is a cathedral at Karies which has the famous wall-paintings, painted by Manuel Panselano in the 14th century and belong to the Macedonian Movement. The icons belong to the Cretan Movement and date back to the 16th century. Amongst the many fascinating wall paintings, the most exquisite ones are, the Birth and Baptism of Jesus, the Holy Virgin, St. John the Evangelist and others.

At the Cathedral, the divine services of the day are conducted by the head supervisor, the supervisors and the representatives from the abbeys of Athos. According to the tradition, the cathedral was built by Great Constantine but was destroyed by Julian the Apostate. In the 10th century it was rebuilt by emperor Nikiphoro Foka only to be destroyed again by Michael Paleologo. It was rebuilt once again by his son Andronicus Paleologos. The miraculous icon «Axion Esti» is kept in the Altar and is always surrounded by the temple's light and the legends.

The Tower

At the southeastern corner of the «Sacred Community's» building and opposite the Protato, lies an ancient tower. Inside the tower, operates the library of Aghion Oros. It accommodates a collection of eighty-two thousand manuscript codes and thousands of prints. Forty-two of the codes are on parchements with excellent minatures. Also, this is the place where the first document of Aghion Oros is kept. It is written on goat skin and that is why it's called Tragos .

In the whole area of Aghion Oros today, and specifically in the small town of Karies, the painting of icons is flourishing. Some of the best-known firms are of the Iosapheon fraternity, of the Pahomeon fraternity, of the Seraphimeon fraternity, of the old and virtuous teacher, Father Meletios Syciotis, of the Archimandrite Damaskenou Rodaki e.t.c.

There is a permanent exhibition of hand-painted icons ▶

Side street at Karies, the capital of Athos.

20

The Fallen. Fresco of Manuel Panselinou. At the Protato (14th century).

at the center of Karies since 1963 which belongs to the Iosepheon fraternity. The exhibition has icons of the Macedonian and Cretan Movements, as well as full-scale copies of icons which belong to the Protato. The icons are noted for their special sense of coloring, their designs and their detailed work. It is obvious that the Iosipheon fraternity is dedicated to a search for excellence. Similar exhibitions also exist at other hagiographical firms of Karies.

Athoniada Ecclesiastical School

The Theologian St. John first operated the School at the Iberian Cell in the 13th century. In 1749 the School was founded again near the abbey of Vatopedi and it was called Academy. The famous Eugene Voulgaris was appointed then as the School-Master. Students who later on became very well-known are Riga Ferreos and Kosmas the Aitolian, while famous teachers were Nephytos, Kaysocalybites, Kyprianos, Athanassios Parios, e.t.c. The School interrupted its operation for a short period but it reopened in 1842.

Since 1930 it operates as a religious seminary and it is supported by the «Sacred Community» while the faculty is paid by the Ministry of Education. Nowadays, it is called Academy

ΗΑΓΙΑ ΓΙΑΣ

▲ Wall - painting in the refectory of Pandokratoros Monastery (1749).

▼ Wall - painting of warrior saints in the refectory of Dionysiou Monastery.

Scenes from the Apocalypse: wall - paintings in the refectory of Dochiariou Monastery (1677)

ОПЕМΠΟС ΑΓΓΕΛΟС ЕСΑΛΠΙСΕ ΚΑΙ ΩΔΑ ΑСΤΕΡΑС ЕΚ ΤΥ ΟΥ ΠΕ ΠΟΚΟΤΑΙС ΓΙΝ ΗΚ ΗΝΟΙΞΕ ΤΟ ΦΡΕ
ΗС ΤΥС ΚΝ ΝΕΒΗ ΚΑΠΝΟС ЕΚ ΤΥ ΦΡΕΑΤ Κ ЕСΚΟΤ СΘΙΟ ΗΛΙΟС ΚΕ ЕΚ ΚΑΠΥ ЕΞΗΛΘΟΝ ΑΚΡΙΔΑС
Κ ЕΔΟΘΗ ΑΥΤΟΙС ЕΞΟΥСΙΑ   ΑΔΙΚΗСΙ ΤΟ СΑΝΟС

and it operates in a wing of St. Andrew's skite.

Saint Andrew's Skite

Five hundred metres northwest of Karies lies St. Andrew's Russian Skite. In the middle of the 18th century monk Vessarios, bought a cell which later on outgrew in buildings and monks and is the largest abbey of Aghion Oros. The central temple of the skite (Katholico) is considered to be the largest in the Balkans, honoring Apostle Andrew's name. It is 60 meters long by 33 meters wide and it's height is 29 meters. The temple was founded in 1867. In the earlier days it used to have 700 Russian monks. It is also called Seragi (palace) because of it's magnificent buildings which the Russians called Sei-rai (paradise). In 1958 the Skite's western end was destroyed by a fire which also burned 20.000 volumes and a large number of manuscripts and antiques. Today the Skite belongs to the Vatopedi abbey. There is only one monk who resides there and he is called Prosmonarios

Koutloumoussiou Abbey

The Koutloumoussiou abbey lies five minutes away to the southwest of Karies. It is situated among huge trees and it is surrounded by hills which are covered with trees. Several cells are spread all around and the natural beauty along with the tranquility that exists there generate unforgettable feelings. There is a spring at the abbey's entrance to quench the visitor's thirst.

The monastery was built before 988 and is considered as one of the oldest abbeys of Athos. It was destroyed later on but at the end of the 13th century it was rebuilt.

The abbeys of Alepiou, Philadelphou and Kaliagras joined the Koutloumoussiou abbey. Soon it became a popular center for intellectual interests and pursuits. In the 15th century it was destroyed by the Pope's latin delegates but it was rebuilt by the Kings of Moldavia and Wallachia. In 1857 and 1870 fires destroyed some wings of the monastery but they were rebuilt thanks to the efforts of the abbot Meletios from Lefkada.

The main temple was built in the middle of the 16th century and it is named in honor of the Transfiguration of Christ. In and out of the monastery, there are thirteen chapels some of which have excellent wall paintings. The reredos of the main temple date from the 19th century and several of the abbey's gems are quite noteworthly and valuable. The library contains 103 manuscripts on parchment, 650 on paper and 3.500 printed.

Skite of St. Panteleimona (Koutloumoussiou)

This Skite which belongs to the Koutloumoussiou abbey

▲ *The Russian skete of St Andrew.*

▼ *The Monastery of St Paul.*

Koutloumousiou Monastery.

consists of nineteen cells and lies near Karies. It was founded in 1785 and its library has a noteworthy collection of manuscripts containing codes and printed matters. The Fathers at the skite are mainly occupied with agriculture, sewing, book-binding, hagiography e.t.c. It is believed that at the location where the skite is built there stood a city during the ancient years.

▶

"Praise Him...": wall - painting in Koutloumousiou Monastery depicting Greek folk instruments.

Carved wooden sanctuary door.

The Vatopediou Abbey

From Karies it takes three hours to go to the big -as it is called- abbey of Vatopedi. On your way to the abbey you pass by wooded valleys and forrests of chestnut-trees mixed with shrubs and wild flowers. The road which is full of turns, climbs several hills and descendes many ridges. It passes through small rivers and crossroads which lead to the monks' hermitages. From time to time, while you continue on the road, you can see the sun trying to come through the clouds. This little game between the sun and the clouds generates a strange feeling of melancholy which is difficult to explain, a longing for something unknown, an invisible nostalgia for what, you don't know. From time to time you can see birds, rabbits and traces of wild boars. At the end of this short, but exhilarating trip you

31

come face to face with the monastery, while further away you can see some additional buildings and the ruins of the old «Athoniada».

The legends say that the monastery was built by Great Constantine but it was destroyed. Later on it was rebuilt by Great Theodosius because he wanted to honor the Virgin Mary who saved his son from drowning by taking him to a bramble (Vato in Greek). That's why the abbey is called Vatopediou (Bramble-child). In 892 it was destroyed by the Arabs and it was rebuilt by three brothers from Adrianoupolis, Nicholas, Athanassios and Antonio. In the 12th century, Serbia's King Symeon and his son Savvas, became monks and came to this particular abbey where they added some buildings. At the beginning of the 14th century and during the invasions of the Catalans, the abbot and ten monks became martyrs after suffering tortures from them. In 1546 the King of Sicily Alphonso, gave to the abbey a document sealed with a golden seal in the Latin language; with this document he imposed a heavy fine to the pirates who might dare to bother the abbey. The kings of Moldavia and Wallachia funded the abbey and so did czar Theodore in 1588.

The main temple of the monastery was built in the 11th century and it is named in honor of Christ's Annunciation. The wall paintings were done in the 14th century but they were renewed in

The Archangel Gabriel.

the 18th century. Inside and outside the monastery there are twenty-eight temples, some of which have excellent wall-paintings.

The Skite of Saint Dimitrios

The skite of Saint Dimitrios, lies thirty minutes away, north of the Vatopedi abbey in a thick forrest. It's main temple (the Kyriako) was decorated with wall paintings and icons in 1755 while it's porch was decorated in 1806. The library contains hand-written and printed matters. The monks are mainly occupied with agriculture and a very small number of them with handi-crafts. There are 15 cells and an equal number of monks. The very well-known cell of St. Procopius is only ten minutes away from the Skite. It was first built in the 11th century surrounded in green-forrest, and its wall paintings belong to the Macedonian Movement.

The Pantokratora monastery.

The Pantokratora Abbey (The Abbey of the Almighty)

This abbey has been built thirty meters above sea level, on a rugged stormbeaten and sun-drenched rock next to the sea. You can go to the abbey by four different ways. From the Vatopedi abbey it takes two hours and a half going on foot or one hour going by sea. From Karies it takes an hour and a half while from the Stavronikita abbey it takes only one hour. Anyhow, all four ways have their own excitement. As soon as you get there you come face to face with a collection of towers, domes, belfries, and cells. This is the Pantokratora abbey. It was built in the middle of the 14th century by two brothers, Alex and John. They were both involved in high rank military positions at their

Dionysiou Monastery: the recess in which the Abbot sits in the refectory

Gold wooden iconostasis of the Prophet Elia cloister.

time and both became monks and died in this abbey, as their will and their mausoleum in the main temple reveals. In 1393 the abbey was burned but was rebuilt with the help of Patriarch Anthony and the emperor Manuel Paleologos. At the beginning of the 15th century or at the end of the 14th, the abbeys of Saint Dimitrios, Afxentiou, Sotiros, Phalakrou and Ravdouhu were annexed to the Pantokratora abbey. Unfortunately, in 1950, the northeastern wing of the monastery was destroyed but it was rebuilt with the help of the Fathers of the Church.

The library contains 317 manuscripts, 68 of which are on parchment (11th-14th century), and the 185 are made of paper. It also contains 4.000 printed matters and a noteworthy collection of Greek stamps. Among the abbey's treasures, we should mention a gospel (0,17 × 0,12) written on a white, thin membrane with miniatures which were possibly painted by John Kalybite, a piece from the shield of St. Mercurius, the piece of wood from the Holy-Cross, the relics of several saints, sacerdotal vestments, e.t.c.

Skite of Prophet Elias

It was founded in 1759 by the Russian monk Paesseo Velitchkofsky. Later on huge buildings and an impressive main temple (which was renovated in

The Stavronikita Monastery.

1900) were added to the first buildings. Amongst its valuable treasures, we can find an excellent holy-bread box, sacerdotal vestments, liturgical objects, crosses, e.t.c.

The abbot and archimandrite Sergio are distinct figures among the monks. It takes an hour to reach the skite from Karies while from the Pantokratora abbey (to which the skite belongs) it takes only twenty-five minutes.

Stavronikita Abbey

You can reach the Stavronikita abbey either by motor-boat from the Pantokratora or the Iveron abbey, or by car from Karies. You can also go there on foot. All around the abbey there are gardens with huge chest-nut trees, like in many other abbeys of Aghion Oros. The abbey was probably founded in the 10th century. In the 11th century, its' tower were used as a watch-tower for the inhabitants of Karies. There are many legends concerning the abbey's foundation. According to one of them, in the earlier days, the Haritona abbey was situated there, or according to another, Stavros and Nikitas established their cells there and that is the reason why the abbey is called

▶

The Palm Holder – Portable icon of the Stavronikita Monastery by Theophanous of Crete (1544).

Life on Mount Athos.

Stavronikitas. In 1533 it was sold as a cell by the Philotheou abbey to abbot Gregory, for 4.000 aspra (coins of a very small value). Under the care of the young abbot at the beginning and of the Patriarch Ieremia (1537-1545) later on the abbey was rebuilt and renamed St. Nicholaos.

In 1607 and 1879, fires destroyed part of the abbey but it was rebuilt with the help of the monks of this and various other abbeys. The many high debts wouldn't allow the monks to make any additions to the buildings or even maintain the existing ones properly until 1960. At the time, the monks finally paid off the debts. In 1968 the abbey was converted into a cenobetic. The main temple has excellent wall-paintings which date from 1546 and it is named in honor of Saint Nicholaos. The wall-paintings were painted according to the Cretan art by the famous artist Theophanes and his son Simeon. The library contains 58 hand-written codes of parchment (11th-14th century), two made of silk, 109 made of paper (14th-19th century) and thousands of prints. Among the altar's wall-paintings we notice the excellent painting of the Lord's Last Supper.

Included in the collection of its treasures are excellent portable icons, crosses, relics of saints, amulets, liturgical objects and a mosaic icon of Saint Nicholaos the Streda which dates

The Iviron Holy Monastery.

Stavronikita Monastery ▶

back to the 14th century. According to legend, this icon was found at the bottom of the sea by some fishermen near the abbey and they gave it to the monks. The icon had an oyster (Strede in Greek) on the saints's forehead and that is why Saint Nicholaos was called Stredas.

Iveron (Iberian's abbey)

Situated in a relaxing and quiet location, the big and famous Iveron abbey is built on the ruins of an ancient city. From Karies it takes one hour and a half to reach the abbey on foot and thirty minutes by car, while from the Stavronikita abbey it takes an hour on foot and fifteen minutes by motor-boat.

Once there, the things you notice are the charming kiosk, a natural cold water-fountain and the impressive portal of its main entrance. As soon as you walk in the front yard, you face the main temple at the center of the yard. At your left hand you see the chapel of Panagia Portaetessa, and at your right hand you can see the library and the vestry. Then comes the Altar, the belfry and archontariki.

During the years of the reign of emperor Michael Paleologos and Patriarch John Beccou, the abbey had the same luck with the Valopedi abbey, because its monks didn't accept to denounce their religions as the latins had asked them to do. After they had been killed they

Outer narthex at the Iviron Monastery.

were thrown into the sea. Some time later the Catalans completed the disaster. In 1357, with a document which was issued by Patriarch Kalistos, the abbey became Greek, not only because of the number of Greek monks which were there, but also because they had a greater contribution from the Iberians in every intellectual endeavour. In the beginning the abbey was cenobetic but in 1880 it became peculiar. Unfortunately, in April 1865, it was completely burned down except for the main temple, but thanks to the efforts of the monks, it was rebuilt. The main temple was built by the Iberian George Varasvatze in 1030, and its wall-paintings were painted between the period of the 16th and the 19th century.

The wall-paintings at the temple's porch represent, not only figures of Saints, but also ancient philosophers like Sophocles, Thoucydides, Platon,

Ploutarch, Aristotle, e.t.c.
During the Greek revolution, in 1821, the abbey sold a large number of its treasures, in order to raise money for the Greek rebels. The last of the iberian monks died in 1955. At the Iveron abbey they operate under the Haldeon time-system which is based on sunset. So, when the sun rises, the time is 0 while for the rest of Athos, time 0 always coincides with sunset.

The abbey has 17 chapels, among them the chapel of Portaetessa where the icon with the same name which works miracles, is devoutly kept. The library is situated in a seperate building. There, we can see 2.000 hand-written codes and about 13.000 prints. From the several treasures of the abbey, we should notice the icon of Portaetessa, the silver candle-stick holder made according to the image of a lemon tree, the mantle of Patriarch Gregory the fifth, the sac of the emperor Tsimiski, a piece of wood from the Holy-Cross, relics of several saints, objects of worship and several other items which are carefully kept in perfect condition by the abbey's monks. Thirteen cells depend on this abbey.

Holy Mary the Portaitissa at the Iviron Monastery.

Cake at the Iviron Monastery for the millenium anniversary.

Skite Timiou (Honest) Prodromou or Iberian

An hour to the west of the Iveron abbey, and two hundred meters above sea level, lies the Greek skite of Prodromos. It is a peculiar one and it was founded in 1779. The Skite's monks are occupied with agriculture, hagiography, wood sculpturing e.t.c.

Philotheous Abbey

In a deep green wood, half an hour away from Katakalou abbey, lies the abbey of Philotheou. From Karies it takes two hours and a half to reach this abbey which is built 300 meters above sea level. The buildings of the abbey, along with the surrounding hills, rivers, wild flowers and the huge one-hundred old trees, form one of the most impressive sights in the whole world.

History mixes with tradition and the facts are not easily distinguished from myths. Anyhow, the legends mention that the monastery was built by St. Philotheos who lived before 972, during the same period with St. Athanassios. At the beginning the abbey was called Fteris abbey. Later on, Nikiphoros Botaneates (1078-1081), added new buildings to the existing one, and offered many treasures to the abbey (amongst them, wood from the Holy-Cross).

In the second ritual of Aghion Oros, the abbey comes in the 13th place. In 1492, Gregorian Leontios Sovereign and his son Alexander renovated the abbey. In 1500, abbot of the abbey was probably the hermit Dionysius who later went to Mount Olympus where he founded another abbey. In 1734,

King of Wallachia Gregory Gicas, gave the abbey a decree sealed with his golden seal.

Unfortunately, in 1871, the abbey was all burned down except the main temple, the altar and the library, but the monks rebuilt it little by little, bringing it to the shape it has today. Its main temple has remarkable wall-paintings which date from 1752 and its name was given in honor of Christ's Annunciation. Among its treasures we notice the arm of St. John Chrysostomos, a gift by Andronicos Paleologos the second, the miraculous icon of Glykofilousa which measures 1,26meters × 0,871, relics of several saints, excellent objects of worship, sacerdotal vestments e.t.c. In the altar there are wall-paintings, painted by Georgi from Crete, in 1540

Altogether, there are twelve cells built in this wooded, remote region and two other ones built in Karies, which all belong to the Philotheou Abbey.

Karakalou Abbey

Right between the two abbeys of Lavras and Iveron, in a wooded area, two hundred meters above sea level, there lies the Greek abbey of Karakalou, half an hour away from shore. The first things one sees arriving at the abbey are the fountain, the vine-arbor and the huge tower. In the yard there are many vine-arbors and orange-trees, a common sight at most of the abbeys of Athos. The visitor will notice the

Filotheou Monastery (above) and Karakalou Monastery (below).

fountains, the oratories, ancient architectural fragments, inscriptions which record Acts of Possesion or other important events which all are compounded in an harmonious way. Furthermore, one will notice the palm-trees of the Gregoriou abbey and the cypresses at the Lavra abbey, orange-trees at the Katakalou abbey and two cypresses at the Gregoriou abbey, which make these abbeys distinct from others.

As soon as the visitor arrives to the «archontariki», he will enjoy a wonderful view. To the east he can see the Aegean sea stretching to meet the sky. To the west there are wild ravines all around the summits of Athos mountains.

We don't know much about how the abbey was built and the legends sound a little bit controversial. Anyway, it is assumed from several documents that were found, that the abbey existed from the 11th century but we still don't know who founded it. According to tradition, the abbey's founder is someone called Nicholaos from the village Karakalla (that's why the abbey is called Karakalou). During the 13th century the abbey was deserted and it was renovated in 1294 by Andronicus Paleologos the second.

At the third ritual of Aghion Oros, it has the third place among the abbeys. Unfortunately, it was destroyed again by the pirates and it was rebuilt in the 16th century by the King of Wallachia, Peter the fifth, who

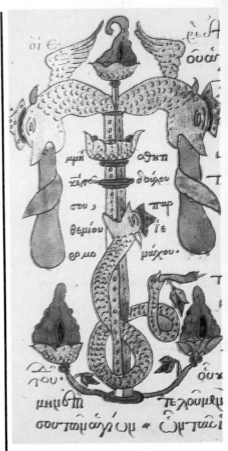

Artistic initial of letter T. from a manuscript.

became a monk. In 1707, Dionysius the Iberian, restored the north wing. In 1877 the south wing was rebuilt, after it was burned the previous year. The east wing was built in 1888. The main temple was built during the period 1548-1563 and its wall-paintings date from the 18th century. The icon of the Twelve Apostles is a painting done by the famous artist Dionysios from Furna (1722). The abbey has seven chapels, four of which

46

have wall-paintings and icons. The abbey's library contains about 300 manuscripts, 42 of which are of parchment and 3.000 prints. The collection of treasures, includes wood from the Holy-Cross, amulets, crosses, relics of saints, sacerdotal vestments, e.t.c.

In the beginning, the abbey was peculiar. In 1813 it became a cenobetic one. 18 cells belong to the abbey, four of them are at Karies and the other fourteen are scattered in the woods.

Monastery of Megisti Lavra.

▲ The Great Laura (aerial photograph).
The south chapel of the main church of Pandokratoros Monastery's skete of the Prophet Elijah

Megistis Lavras Abbey

At the southeastern part of Aghion Oros, where the Athos mountain gently slides down to the sea, in 963, Athanassios the Athonian founded the Megistis Lavras abbey. The emperor Nikiphoros Phokas provided the money for this ambitious plan, in order to help his friend Athanassios to gather the hermits at this abbey. A king's order secured regular funding for the abbey from the island of Limnos, as well as from Peristeron abbey at Thessaloniki, which also joined the abbey of Lavra.

The main temple dates back to the 10th century. Its excellent wall-paintings which date back to the beginning of the 16th century were painted by the famous artists Theophanes from the island of Crete. At one of the abbey's chapels which is named in honor of the Forty Saints, lies the grave of St. Athanassios, who's memory is celebrated on the fifth of July. The Saint's relic is in a coffin and seven oil-candles are lit near by day and night. In the same chapel, two rare icons are kept. One of them is the one of Jesus Christ while the other, is of the Virgin Mary who is called here Economissa .

Besides the main temple, Lavras abbey has thirty-seven smaller temples. In the temple of St. Athanassios, we can see the iron rod with which St. Athanassios, crossly hit a stone, and as legend tells us, water poured from it. We can also see his iron cross, which weighs four kilos and which St. Athanassios kept hanging from his neck while he conducted his long divine services. Another important chapel is the one of Koukousellisas, where the famous miracle involving the choir-leader John Koukouselli took place in the 12th century. To the west of the main temple's entrance, stands the altar which has very important wall-paints and an excellent decoration. It is divided in three zones. In the first one we can read the 24 verses of a famous hymn. In the middle one we can see several scenes from the life and tortures of the monks and at the lower zone we can see the full frames of saints, monks and hermits, who are highly honored by the monks of Athos.

We can also see here the root of Iessai, the «ancient sages», Thales, Solon, Socrates, Philon, Galenos, Cleanthes, Aristotle and others. The main characteristic of these pictures is that they are high-lighted by bright coloring and tones.

The treasury and the wealthy library lie behind the main temple. There, knowledge and treasures from every possible source are gathered in order to enlighten the future generations. In the vestry we can see among the other treasures, the sac of emperor Nikiphoros Phokas, which weighs six kilos, and has precious stones and roses of many colors. The emperor's crown, a gospel decorated with precious stones, portable mosaic icons, a quiver with poison arrows fron ancient years, a piece of wood from the Holy-Cross, relics of several saints, riffles from the Greek Revolution of 1821 against the Turks, amulets, chalices, wood sculptured icons, sacerdotal vestments, e.t.c. The library contains 2.200 codes, 470 of them are on parchments (10th-14th century), 50 on membranes and 10.000 prints.

Also situated there, are the graves of three Patriarchs and hundreds of portable icons of great value which are kept in reserve for a chapel near the grave-sight. Today, the abbey is a peculiar one. On the first day of every month a sanctification is conducted between the main

Jesus Christ and his eight angelic orders. Fresco at the Chapel of Coucouzelisa at the Monastery of Megisti Lavra. 18th century.

temple and the altar. The Skites of St. Anne, Kafsocalybion, Timiou Prodromou (Rumanian), the small skite of St. Anne, Carulia, Catunakia, St. Basil and Provata all belong to the abbey of Lavra.

The Desert

Between the abbeys of Lavra and St. Paul, six hours away on foot, stretches the desert, a rocky, barren and unfriendly place, which became the residence of thousands of hermits for many years and continues even today. The hermits live alone, because they believe that co-habitation doesn't allow them to concentrate on their religious endeavours. When you see this desert, in the tranquillity and calmness of an autumn night you can easily remember the hermits of the Egyptian desert.

Skite Timiou Prodromou (Rumanian)

An hour away from the abbey of Lavra, and on a hill about 250 meters from the sea, lies this Rumanian Skite. This cenobetic skite, was built in 1857. It was founed by the monks Nectarios and Nephona and it is named in honor of St. John Prodromos. The temple has relatively recent wall-paintings. Today the skite has only a hand-full of monks.

Kafsocalybion Skite (The Skite of the burned huts)

Three hours away from the abbey of Lavra, and one hundred meters above sea level, lies this skite high on the rocks. The skite's main temple which is called Kyriako was built in 1745 and its wall-paintings were painted at the end of the 18th century. The library contains twenty-three codes and a few hundred prints. At the skite we can also see a collection of treasures, which contains sacerdotal vestments, icons, crosses, relics of saints, e.t.c.

The Karoulia

This is the main area of the hermits, a barren, rocky and rugged place where the hermits live in huts and the ascetics in caves. The name of the area comes from the pulley which the hermits use to hang the basket where the passing fishermen put a piece of bread in and whatever they have available. The same basket is used by the hermits to pay the fishermen with their handicrafts. Here the slope's gradient is 90-95%. There, the monks have built twelve small huts. To some of them you can descend by chains of scalling-ladders while for the others which are more like caves than huts, you have to find the right and sometimes invisible path in the rocks.

In order to gather vegetables or find water, the hermits have to

51

climp up and down precipices. Their food consists mainly of vegetables, rusks, prickly pears and dry food. They get very little sleep, but they study a lot and pray continuously. They rarely talk, but their faces have a special brightness. They carefully listen to people's worries and troubles and they seem to care a great deal.

The Catunakia

High up on the summit lies the mamous hagiographical firm of Danieleon which is called by the pilgrims Oasis in the desert . Formaly, it is a cell but it really is a small abbey. The monks are occupied with hagiography and they have offered hundreds of their paintings to several orthodox churches all over the world. This firm was founded seventy years ago by the scholar monk Daniel, under the supervison of the abbey of St. Panteleimona. Furthermore, the contribution of the fraternity to Byzantine music is great and they don't hesitate to praise the Lord when are invited by the other monks to the festivals of Aghion Oros.

St. Anne's Skite

Five hours away from the abbey of Lavra and one hour away from St. Paul's abbey, lies the skite of St. Anne. It is situated in a real oasis with thick vegetation. The skite –which is the oldest and largest in Aghion

Sight of a hermitage.

Oros– was founded in the 16th century and today consists of nearly fifty cells and huts. Near the sea, one can notice the ruins of the very old Voulefterion abbey. The monks are pre-occupied by painting, handicrafts and agriculture.

All the monks of Aghion Oros are people with intellect and interests and altruistic attitudes, therefore it is not strange that the monks of St. Anne's skite share their food with the hermits who live high on the rocks of Carulia.

The skite's main temple (Kyriako) is named in honor of St. Anne and was built by Patriarch Dionysus Vardale in 1666. From 1752 until 1755 the temple expanded and its wall-paintings were painted. The library contains three codes made of parchment, two hundred manuscripts and seven hundred prints. The famous writer of hymns Gerasimos Gerasimakis was in charge of the library's

52

St. Anna. Fresco.

equipment. Some of the important hagiographical firms are the firm of the Katsona brothers and the one of the old Ananias and others.

The Nea (New) Skite

The Nea Skite is built on a flat area near the sea. It was occupied in 1760 and belongs to the abbey of St. Paul. It consists of about thirty seven cells and huts. The sixty, (more or less) monks are occupied with hagiography, music, agriculture, the sculpturing of icons on wood and with golddigging and elaborating gold. At the library of «Kyriako» we can see twenty hand-written codes, five hundred prints, sacerdotal vestments, crosses, relics of saints, etc. The skites hagiographical firms of Kyrileon, Abrameon, Halderon, Gerontos, Varlaam and others are considered as important in their kind. The person who is in charge for the hospitality of the visitors and for keeping the place clean, is called 'Deakeos' and he is elected each year. He corresponds for the public affairs of the monks and he takes care of the performances of the divine services in the 'kyriako', every Sunday. At this skite, the artist and monk Callestos lives an ascetic life. His work is distinguished for this inspiration and realistic attitude.

St. Paul's Abbey

Between two torrents, twenty minutes away from the sea, lies the cenobetic abbey of St. Paul, situated midway between the Nea Skite and the Dionysiou abbey. It is built forty meters above sea level and according to legends, it was founded in the 8th century. Anyway, evidences for the abbey's existence date back to the 10th century, when abbot of the abbey was Paul the Xeropotamenos. Paul, along with the First of Aghion Oros (the Supervisor), was sent to emperor John Tsimiski, in order to denounce Athanassios the Athonian for the innovations he established in Aghion Oros.

Another legend states that at the very same place where this abbey is built, existed another one which was devoted to the Presentation of the Virgin Mary and which was built by the ascetic Stephen in 337. Anyway, the abbey and its limits are mentioned in a document (1257) issued by emperor Michael Paleologos. At the third ritual of Aghion Oros, the abbey comes

Nea Skete, which belongs to the Monastery of St Paul.

in the 18th place.

The abbey was destroyed in the 14th century, probably by the Catalans (1309). As a result, it became a cell and in 1360 it was sold by the Sovereign abbey of Xeropotamou, to the Serbian monks Gerasimos and Anthony. Since then, the abbey's renovators and benefactors are all kings from Serbia, Moldavia and Wallachia. Among them, George Vragovin, who built the old main temple and his daughter Maro, wife of the Sultan Murat the second, and mother of Porthetu, who offered to the abbey part of the offerings which the three Magi had offered to the infant Jesus Christ. In 1817, the monks rebuilt the ruined main temple and they decorated in with marbles from the quarries of Tenos, Penteli and Aghion Oros, under the guidance of the craftsman Lyrite from Tenos.

The library contains 492 manuscripts, 13.000 prints, imperial and ecclesiastical documents, hand-written messages from the Patriarch, etc. Also, hundreds of documents, mainly concerning Turkish and Slavonian offerings, are kept there. Among the collection of valuables, we can see wood from the Holy-Cross, a part of the offerings of the three Magi to the infant Jesus, valuable icons, golden covers for gospels, Silver and enamel amulets, crosses, several objects of worship, diptychs, a portable painting on glass which dates

Main church of Saint Paul's Monastery.

back to the 13th century and shows the Lord's Prayer and others.

Today, the abbey has 45 monks and 80 dependants. The abbey also has 10 chapels, and amongst them is that one of St. George with wall-paints which date back to the 16th century.

The abbey is considered as one of the most strict cenobetic abbeys in Athos.

The Skite of St. Dimitrios or Skite of Laccou (Pit)

At the northeastern part of Athos lies the skite of Laccou, which belongs to St. Paul's abbey. It was built in the 18th century, two hundred meters above sea level. The Kyriako

was built in 1900. Today it has about twenty huts where the Rumanian monks live an ascetic life.

Dionysiou Abbey

The abbey of Dionysiou is built 80 meters above sea level on a huge and rugged rock. To the west of the abbey flows the torrent Aeropotamos. The cells of the monks face the sea and they have balconies all around. Between them, there is a somewhat narrow yard in the centre of which stands the abbey's main temple. It is named in honor of Prodromos whose memory is celebrated on August 29th. The whole unit consists of a huge tower (which used to be

55

Dionysiou Monastery.

Grigoriou Monastery.

A scene from the Book of Revelations. Monastery of Dionysiou. – 17th century.

a watch-tower) and many other buildings all around. The 'archondariki' lies at the north wing of the abbey while the cells are at the south wing. Externally, the abbey looks like a fortress. When you look down from Tarsana at the abbey's side, it looks like it consists of hanging arcades made of wood, which crown the rugged summits of the rocks. To the east and near the abbey's grave-yeard lies the grave of St. Nephona Patriarch of Constantinople, while to the west, there are wild ravines which echo under the north wind.

The abbey was built in 1839 by monk Dionysius from Koresso of Kastoria. His brother, who was the abbot of the Philotheou abbey, became Metropolitan of Trevizond which emperor Alexios Commenos the third valued a great deal.

When the abbey was burned, Dionysius went to Trebizond to visit his brother. As a result, the emperor offered many treasures for the abbey of Dionysius and granted an annual contribution. He also wished that the abbey would be called 'abbey of the Great Comnenos'.

Interest for this abbey was also expressed by the Dynasty of Paleologos as well as by the kings of Wallachia, Radopoulos and Neagos Basarabas. The latter, in 1510, built the tower and the aqueduct. In 1533, the abbey was burned again, but the king of Moldavia and Wallachia Pierre rebuilt it. He also rebuilt the main temple which was finished in 1547, with excellent wall-paintings, painted by the famous Cretan artist Georgi. At the third ritual of Aghion Oros, the abbey comes in the 19th place among the twenty five abbeys, which existed at that time. In 1574, when the Xeropotamou abbey was burned, it took its place and now it is fifth in line. The altar which lies to the southwest of the main temple has icons painted by Mercurius and Daniel, which date back to 1603. The library contains 126 hand-written codes of parchment, 11 of silk, 661 of paper and 5.500 prints, (among them 45 original and old copies). Some of the manuscripts have remarkable miniatures.

Among the many treasures of the abbey we can see gospels crosses, amulets, excellent reliquaries, portable icons, embroidered sacerdotal vestments, etc. Seven cells belong to the abbey.

Gregoriou Abbey

Between the abbeys of Simonopetras and Dionysiou, lies the Gregoriou abbey, built on a rugged rock twenty meters above sea level. The sea-route between the abbeys of Gregoriou and Dionysiou is full of excitement. Rocky, rugged coast succeds idyllic beaches while one can easily notice the wild precipies and the steep slopes all around. The monks keep the interior of the abbey all-white all year around. The balconies of the 'archondariki' form a little paradise for the visitors. They can hear the roar of the waves all day and night while sweet breezes come from the nearby ravine. The abbey -as one of its hand-written coes (number 34) reveals- was founded at the beginning of the 14th century by St. Gregory the Sinaiti. At the third ritual of Aghion Oros the abbey comes in the 22nd place among the twenty five abbeys.

In 1497, it was deserted and in 1500 it was renovated by Wallachia's Kind Stepen, father of Bogdan Voivoda, and under the care of abbot Spyridona. Unfortunately, it was burned in 1761, but it was rebuilt by the sexton Ioakim Macrigeni. He was the one who asked for contributions from the kings of Wallachia, from Gregory who was at the Cathedral of Hungary and Wallachia, and from Phanariots (members of the Greek official class under the Turks).

In 1821, the monks of the

ὉΠΡΟ ΔΝΙ ΗΛ ΕΝ ΤΛΑΚΟ ῶΝ ΛΕΟΝ ῶΝ.   ἩΓΙΣΠΕΛΕC

Daniel in the bin with the Lions. Fresco in the Gregoriou Monastery 1739.

Gregoriou abbey, helped the rebels by offering them valuable items from their treasure collections. Until 1840 the abbey was a peculiar one. Since then it is one of the most strict cenobetic abbeys in Aghion Oros. The wall paintings of its main temple date back to 1779. This is where the unique manuscript of the 'Shepherd of Herma' is kept. In the abbey there are twelve chapels, among them the Kemeteriou one with excellent wall-paintings. The main temple is named in honor of St. Nicholas and its wall-paintings date back to the 18th century. Some of the noteworthy valuables are the crosses, the amulets, the precious stones, the relics of saints, the gospels, the gold embroidered epitaphs from the 15th century and the imperial and ecclesiastical documents.

The Abbey of Simonos Petras

It takes one hour travelling on foot to reach the abbey of Simonos Petras, which dominates the area. It is built two hundred and thirty meters above sea level on a slope of the wooded mountain.

The blue color of the usually calm sea and the green of the mountain harmonize perfectly with the dark colors of the sea-drenched rocks. The cliff on which the abbey is built seems as if hanging over the sea, apart

The Simonos Petra Monastery.

from the rest of the mountain. The abbey way up there, looks quite impressive. When the visitor stands on the highest balcony of this seven-story building, he thinks that he's travelling over the sea by plane.

On this big and rugged cliff, St. Simeon, guided by a light which was sent by God, built his abbey in the middle of the 14th century. It is said that when the abbey was being built, Simeon's attendant, monk Isaiah, slipped from the high scaffold he was walking on. He rolled down the ravine, but when he reached its bottom, he was standing on his feet. His faith had saved him and that miracle gave the courage to the other workers to go on with the work. In 1364, the abbey expanded by the help of Serbia's King John Uglesi, who sent many treasures with the Supervisor Efthymios, in order to fund the abbey's building. At the third ritual (1394), of Aghion Oros, it comes in the third place among the twenty five abbeys. In 1580 and 1626, it was burned down. It was a peculiar abbey until 1801 when it became cenobetic. Unfortunately, it was completely burned down again 1891, but the monks, under the commands and guidance of abbot Neophytos and with great effort, rebuilt the abbey, and added a new wing.

Apart from the main temple, there are eight chapels in and out of the abbey. Nowadays, the abbey is a cenobetic one and its

St George: wall - painting in Xiropotamou Monastery.

treasures consists of wood from the Holy-Cross, sacerdotal vestments, amulets, icons and relics of saints.

The Xeropotamou (Dry River) Abbey

Two hundred meters from the sea, east of the abbey of St. Panteleimona and west of the Simonos petras abbey lies the beautiful abbey of Xeropotamou which is built in a wooded area. According to tradition, ancient Horadria was built there or even probably the little town of Kleonas.

The abbey's name comes from the nearby dry riverbed, and its buildings dominate the area of the Sigiticos bay.

According to tradition, in 424, at the same place, Poulcheria, sister of Emperor Theodosius Micros and wife of

The preparation of the Trhone, Fresco at the Monastery Xiropotamou – 1783.

Emperor Marcianos, built the Chimarou (torrent) abbey. This abbey changed its name later (we don't know when) and it was named Xeropotamou abbey. It is also said that it was burned down by the Saracens but Emperor Constantine Porfyrogenitos the seventh (912-959) and Romanos A΄ Lekapinos (914-944) rebuilt the abbey.

Movreover, Porfyrogenitos (means born in red) offered to the abbey a sumptuous red mantle, to be worn by the abbot during the feast-days, as Romanos offered a big piece of wood from the Holy-Cross.

Nowadays, we can still notice marble inscriptions at the entrance of the ruined tower of the abbey, which are relative to the contributions of the above emperors. The written traditions state that the abbey was built by Paul Xeropotameno in the

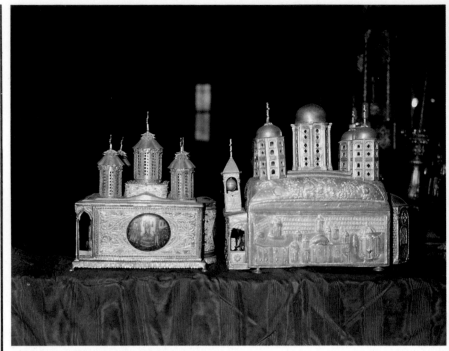

Shrines at Xiropotamou Monastery.

second half of the 10th century and after Lavras abbey had been built, as the first ritual of Aghion Oros states. Paul became the first abbot of the abbey. He was an ascetic man, with intellectual interests and he showed a great traditionalism. In the 11th century, the abbey expanded considerably on the south side of the peninsula, and its boundaries reached the abbey of St. Paul (which according to tradition was also founded by Paul the Xeropotameno). In 1280 the abbey was destroyed but not only was it rebuilt by Emperor Andronicus Paleologos, the second, but he also secured the abbey's land with a document

sealed with his golden seal (1302).

In 1507, it was burned but was rebuilt again with the efforts of the abbey's monks and the contribution of Sultan Selim the first (1514-1519) who also benefited the whole community of Aghion Oros by issuing the Hatti-Serif (Sacred Definition).

In 1609, half of the abbey was burned and plundered by pirates, but was soon rebuilt with the help of Wallachia's King Alexander. The 17th and 18th centuries were quite tough for the monks. At that time, the abbey lost its fifth place in the hierachy of the abbeys and slipped to the eigth place. In

Monastery Xiropotamou – Second coming of Christ. Fresco 1783.

1760 the abbey was renovated by the prolific author and erudite monk of the abbey Caesario Daponte, from Scopelos. At the same time, the main temple was also built. It is thirty meters long, nineteen meters wide and fifteen meters high. It was decorated with excellent scenes from the Old and New Tesament

Today, the abbey has a three-story square shaped building. It is a peculiar abbey. It is named in honor of the Forty Saints and celebrates their memory on the 9th of March. Except its main temple, the abbey has twelve chapels. Among the abbey's treasures we can notice the four pieces of wood from the Holy-Cross, one of which is a present from Emperor Romano and it is the biggest known piece in the world (0,13×0,16 mm). At the bottom of this piece there is an engraving which is tilled with a red diamond and twelve other precious stones. Furthermore, we can see a small tray made of steatite which, as they say, is a present by Empress Pulcheria, four sceptres of bishops (two of them are made of amber), part of the Magi's offerings to the infant Jesus, a piece of the Thorny Wreathe, pieces of the sponge and the mantle of Jesus, 61 relics of Saints, precious sacerdotal vestments embroidered with gold, crosses, gospels, liturgical objects, portable icons, documents and others. Its library, which is situated over the narthex, contains three hundred and forty manuscripts and four hundred prints. Unfortunately, half of the abbeys' south wing was burned in 1969.

St. Panteleimonos Abbey

Going by motor-boat from the Xenofontos abbey and just before we reach Dafne, we can see the Russian abbey of St. Panteleimonos. It is built in a wooded area next to the sea. It is a cenobetic abbey and it celebrates on the 27th of July. When you look at it from a distance, it looks like a fort with lots of domes and windows.

Going towards Karies and half an hour away on a plateau,

Main Temple at Saint Panteleimona Monastery.

lies the Paliomonastero (old abbey) which depends on St. Panteleimonos abbey since 1765.

At this place the Thessalonikeos abbey was first built, which later on lost its importance and was deserted. For this reason, during the 12th century, the First of Aghion Oros, along with his followers offered the deserted abbey to the Xelurgu abbey which was inhabited by Russian monks and which nowadays is called Vogodoritsa. The monks of Xelurgu went to the deserted abbey and the Xelurgu became a Skite (1168). During the 13th century it was burned, along with all the documents which were kept there.

For this reason Andronicos Paleologos (1282-1328) secured the abbeys' land by issuing a documents sealed with his golden seal. For the next one hundred years, it was continuously under the protection of the Serb Kings. From 1314 the abbey is called St. Panteleimonos abbey of the Russians.

The Paleologos dynasty first and the Serbian Kings later, benefited the abbey by providing gems and land. At the Third Ritual of Aghion Oros the abbey comes fifth at the hierarchy of the abbeys. The abbot used to sign the various documents in Greek which means that most of the monks were Greek. The abbey had a lot of Russian

Above: Xiropotamou Monastery. Below: Pandeleimonos Monastery.

monks after the year 1497. In 1552 it seems that it closed down temporarily but it soon operated again with a few monks. Anyhow, the 17th century, was a declining one for the abbey. In 1725 the abbey had two Russian and two Bulgarian monks. In the middle of the 18th century the abbey was occupied by Greeks. A bit later the monks left permanently and came near the sea along the area where lerissu Christoforos had built in 1667 the small church which was named in honor of Christ's Resurrection. There, in 1765, they founded the new abbey which was called Russico (Russian).

The abbey's buildings soon multiplied with the help of King Scarlatos Kallimachi and the protection of the Patriarch Gregory the fifth. In 1803, Kallinicus the Fifth, made the abbey a cenobetic one, while in 1839 the Russian monks started coming and some time later it had about two thousand.

Nowadays, it has only a few monks and the divine services are conducted in the Greek and Russian language. The main temple of the abbey was built during the period 1812-1820. It has thirty-five chapels, amont them the temple of the Skepis of Theotokou (the Holy Protector, Virgin Mary), the temple of Alexander Niefske (1852) at the northwest side, and that one of St. metrophanes which is situated west of the library. The altar was built in 1890 and accomodates 800-1000 monks. The belfry (1893) Is over the altar's entrance. Its large bell -the second largest in the world- has a periphery for 8,71 m., a diameter of 2,71 m and it takes two monks to handle its 13,000 Kilos. Furthermore, two other monks, ring in a rhythmical way the other thirty two smaller bells.

The library contains 1064 hand-written codes of leather and paper, and 25.000 Greek and Slavonian prints. The treasures are kept in the abbeys' vestry. Among them we can see wood from the Holy Cross, portable icons, excellent sacerdotal vestments, relics of Saints, several liturgical objects made of gold and silver, icons decorated with precious stones, crosses etc.

Attachments to St. Panteleimonos Abbey

The following monastic foundations belong to St. Panteleimonos abbey.) The Paliomonastero, 2) The cenobetic Bulgarian Skite Vogoritsa (or Xelurgu) which is built on the land that belongs to the Pantokratora abbey 3) the cenobetic skite Chrumitsa (or Gurnoskite). 4) The skite of Neas Thebaedas which is located between the skite of Chrumitsa and the Zographou abbey, and 5) a cell at Karies. Almost all of the skites are ruined. Moreover, the Kyriako of the Neas Thebaedas skite -which would be the largest temple in Aghion Oros- never integrated.

The Crucifixion: wall - painting in Grigoriou Monastery.

Aerial photograph of Xenofondos Monastery.

Xenophontos Abbey

Between the abbeys of Dohiariou and St. Panteleimonos lies the Xenophontos abbey, which is built on a wooded area next to the sea. The abbey is a cenobetic one and it celebrates the memory of St. George on the 23rd of April. Tradition mentions that it was built in 580 by Xenophon the Siglitico, but according to some written testimonies it was built in the 10th century by Xenophon. He was acquainted with Athanassius the Athonian because the latter had cured Xenophons' brother of an incurable disease.

The old main temple has excellent wall-paintings, painted by Anthony, an artist of the Cretan movement (1544). The altars' wall-paintings were painted in the 16th century. The reredos of the new main temple are made of marble. This temple is bigger and much more impressive than the other main temples of Aghion Oros. There, we can see two mosaic icons of St. Dimitrios and St. George and a smaller one of the Transfiguration of Christ which all date back to the 14th century.

Nowadays, it has eleven chapels there, of which still have icons. The belfry is in a square tower which was built in 1864, while the fountain with the cover in front of the tower was built in 1908. The library contains 300 manuscripts and 3.500 prints. The treasures comprise of wood

The Dochiariou Monastery.

from the Holy Cross, portable icons, liturgical objects, relics of several saints, mosaic icons and others.

Xenophon's Skite

From the abbey of Xenophon and going northeast, it takes an hour on foot to reach Xenophon's skite which was founded in 1766 by the priest and monk Sylvester and by the old men Agapio and Euphrem. It consists of nearly fifteen huts and the Kyriako which was built in the same year. The narthex was rebuilt in 1901 by the monks. The library contins 360 hand-written codes and 550 prints. The gems comprise sacerdotal vestments, crosses, icons, relics of saints and others.

Dohiariou Abbey

Thirty meters above sea level and between the abbeys of Xenophontos and Constamonetou, lies the peculiar abbey of Dohiariou, built at the foot of a wooded slope. This is a Greek abbey and it celebrates the memory of the Archangels Michael and Gabriel on the 8th of November.

It was built by monk Efthymios who was a storehouse-Keeper (Dohiaris) at Lavra during the 11th century. Also mentioned is the name of Patrikios Nicolaos who became monk under the name Neophytos. It seems that he was a nephew of Efthymios. The abbey received many

wooden iconostasis at the Dochiariou Monastery.

benefits from the emperor Michael the 7th the Ducas 1071-1078) and his mother Evdocea. In the beginning the abbey was built somewhere around Dafne but later was rebuilt by the same founder at the same place where it is situated today. At the second ritual of Aghion Oros the abbey comes in the 10th place among the 180 abbeys which existed then, while at the third ritual it comes in the 11th place among the 25. Later the monks deserted the abbey becaus of the pirates, but it was rebuilt in 1578, by priest George from Adrianopoles and it was renovated by Moldavia's king Alexander and his wife Roxane. At the same time also, the main temple was built, and it was decorated with

◄

The Persecutions of various Saints. Fresco.

The Family Tree of Iesse. Fresco in the Dochiariou Monastery.

excellent wall-paintings of the Cretan movement. The ex-metropolitan of Moldavia Theophanes -who was retired from his duties and became monk in this abbey- is burried here. In the 17th and 18th centuries new wings were added and a belfry was built. The noteworthy reredos and the excellent sculptured box of wood in the altar were made during 1783.

Nowadays the abbey has ten chapels, and several of them have wall-paintings. The altar was built by Ahrida's archbishop Prochoro and was decorated with wall-paintings in 1700. The library, which is located on the second floor of the tower, contains 441 hand-written codes and about 2.000 prints. Sixty-five of the codes are on parchment.

At the abbey we also find the sanctification of the Archangels Michael and Gabriel. Among it treasures we can see the icon of Gorgoepicou, wood from the Holy-Cross, portable icons, objects of worship, sacerdotal vestments, relics of 45 saints and others.

Constamonetou Abbey

The Constamonetou abbey lies in a picturesque location, 200 meters above sea level. It is built in a green wood, forty five minutes away from the coast. According to tradition it was founded by Great Constantine but was integrated by his son Constans. Another tradition states that the abbey was built by a hermit who was born in Castamona of Paflagonia. Anyway according to the historical sources, it was built in the 11th century. At the beginning of the 14th century it was burned by the Catalans but it was sson rebuilt. In 1351, emperor John Paleologos the first defined the abbeys' land by issuing a document sealed with his golden seal. In 1360, princess Anne the Philanthropist and George Vrancovits gave many donations to the abbey. In 1393, at the third ritual of Aghion Oros it is mentined as Constantinou abbey. Later on the abbey was burned but was renovated in 1433, by Serbia's Commander in Chief Radits who became a monk there, under the name Romanos. The abbey had its declining years at the end of the 16th century and it became a cenobetic abbey. In 1820, part of the abbey was built, with a donation from the wife of Ali

The Constamonitou Monastery.

Pasha, Basiliki. In 1853, two monks from Xenophon's skite came to reside there and funded the abbey. In 1870, the main temple and a wing were rebuilt by contributions from Russia. Nowadays, there are five chapels in the abbey. The library which is situated over the narthex, contains 110 manuscripts, among them an erased and rewritten code of the 12th century and two illustrated gospels of the 11th century. The treasure collection contains wood from the Holy Cross, portable icons, embroidered sacerdotal vestments, objects of worship, several documents etc.

Zographou Abbey

This Bulgarian cenobetic abbey is built 160 meters above sea level. It is situated in a forrest near a ravine, an hour away from the coast.

It is said that the abbey was

The well and the tower of Filotheou Monastery.

Athonite cells.

Karoulia: a place of harsh ascesis.

The iconography workshop of the Daniilaion fraternity.

St Athanasius: wall - painting in the Monastery of St Paul.

The Zographou Monastery.

built during the years of Leontos Sophou, in the 9th century, by the brothers Moses, John and Aaron from Ahrida. It was called abbey of St. George the painter. At the third ritual of Aghion Oros, the abbey comes in the 10th place among the abbeys of Aghion Oros. In the 13th century it must of had Bulgarian monks because it also was called abbey of the Bulgarians. In the same period, the abbey was funded by Michael Paleologos the eigth. At the beginning of the 14th century, the abbey was burned by the Catalans and they tortured many monks. In the period of the disputes between those who wanted the unity of the Catholic and Orthodox churches and those who didn't the monks vigorously opposed to the union. As a result, the followers of the idea of unity, burned 26 monks in the abbeys' towere. There, in 1873, the monks raised a cenotaph for

Chelandariou Monastery. Southeast wing.

these fearless faithfulls. The abbey received many benefits from Andronicos Paleologos the second, Andronicos Paleologos the third and John as well as from the Kings of Serbia, Moldavia and Wallachia. In 1502, after it was deserted, the King of Moldavia and Wallachia Stephen the sixth Kalos, renovated it.

In 1716, the abbeys' east wing was repaired and in the period 1862-1896 the north and the west side of the abbey were built. Earlier, there were at the abbey Serbian, Bulgarian and Greek monks, therefore the divine services were conducted both in the Greek and the Bulgarian language. Since 1845, the Bulgarians outnumber the other monks of this abbey which is a cenobetic one since 1850.

The new main temple was built in 1801 and its wall-paintings were painted in 1817. The reredos and the altar are made of wood and they are excellently sculptured. Three of the 14 chapels which belong to the abbey have icons. The library which is situated in the tower contains 550 hand-written codes.

Of these, 162 are in the Greek language and 388 in the Slavonian. It also contais 16.500 prints. The treasure collection consists of relics of saints, sacerdotal vestments, liturgical objects, icons that perform miracles, historical documents and others. In the 18th century, in this same abbey lived monk

Paesios, historian of the Bulgarian history. At the same area we can see the hut where Cosmas the Aetolean lived a monastic life.

Helandariou Abbey

The impressive Serbian abbey of Helandariou, lies in a wooded area, fifty meters above sea level, and at some distance from the sea. It celebrates the Presentation of Virgin Mary on the 21st of November. Its' name comes from the founder of a small abbey who was called Hilandarios or Helandarios Ratskos, the son of the Serbian King Stephen Nemania, who came to Athos where he became a monk at the St. Panteleimonos abbey, under the name Savvas. His decision, shocked his father -who was the son-in-law of emperor Alexiou Angelou the third- and he followed him to Aghion Oros. There King Stephen became monk under the name Simeon. Later, at the request of Serbia's new king, Stephen the second, Emperor Alexios Comnenos the third offered to the Serbian monks the ruined abbey of Helandariou which belonged to the Vatopedi abbey, and confirmed the offer by issuing a document, sealed with his golden seal. There, the two monks built the Helandari (or Hilandari) which as is said, means some kind of ship. They enriched the abbey with treasures and gems and from the beginning of the 13th century they developed it into an intellectual and religous center for their people.

Later on, Savvas became the archbishop of Servia. When the two monks died, they were proclaimed Saints. Their graves are located to the northeast of the main temple.

During the following years, the abbey received many benefits and treasures from the Serbian Kings and in that way, it acquired the largest -next to Lavra's- share of land in the Athos peninsual.

The small abbeys of Scorpios, Comitissa, Kalica, Strovilea and the fourth in the hierarchy abbey of Zigos were annexed to the Helandariou abbey, which then became fourth in the hierarchy. In 1722 and 1891, after the visit of the Serb King Alexander Ovrenovits, many Serbian monks enrolled in this abbey. When Macedonia was emancipated (in 1913) the Serb monks strongly favoured the unity of Aghion Oros with Greece. Nowadays, the abbey comes in the fourth place among the abbeys and it has about twenty five monks. The main temple was built in the 13th century. Its' wall-paintings were painted in the 14th century but they painted it again in the 19th century and the excellent wall-paintings of the Macedonian movement were destroyed. The mosaics on the floor and the wooden and sculptured reredos (which date from 1774) are the best of their kind, in Aghion Oros. Among the tewlve chapels of the abbey, only St. George's has wall paintings.

St Mercurius: wall - painting by Manuel Panselinos in the Protaton (14th c.).

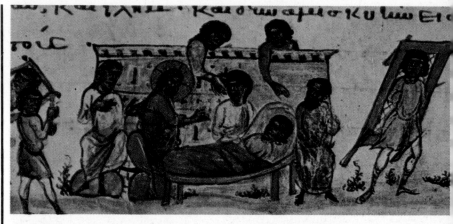

Jesus Christ healing sick. Small painting on a manuscript.

The library contains 800 manuscripts and 7.000 prints. The altars wall-paintings were painted 1623. Among the treasures which are kept in the vestry (which was recently decorated) we can see two crosses made of wood from the Holy Cross, another one with precious stones, sceptres, embroideries, excellent portable icons, banners of kings, coin collections, objects of worship, icons, historical documents, engravings on copper and many others.

Attachments to the Abbey

Fifteen cells, in and out of Karies, belong to the Helandariou abbey. Among them the cell of Molybdoclesias which has excellent wall-paintings of the Cretan artist Georgi (1536-1541) and a remarkable wooden and sculptured reredos which dates back to the 17th century.

Esphigmenou Abbey

The famous and impressive abbey of Esphigmenou is situated in a peaceful location near the sea. Its name originates from its position as it is Squeezed in as it seems by two mountains. (Sphigmeno in Greek means to squeeze).

Some others say that its name originates from its founder who had a tight rope around his waist (Sphigmenos). According to tradition, the abbey (which celebrates the Ascension of Christ) was built by Theodosius the Micros and his sister, empress Poulheria (408-450) who was Marciano's wife. Still according to tradition, later on the abbey was destroyed by a huge rock which fell from the mountain. The ruins of the old abbey are situated half a kilometer away. The new abbey was built at the end of the 10th century or at the begining of the 11th century by the monks of the old abbey.

Anyhow, the first written document for the abbey is a letter from Paul the Xeropotamite

The Esfigmenou Monastery.

◄ *The Dormition of the Virgin: portable icon in Stavronikita Monastery.*

written in 1001. For a short period in the 14th century, abbot of the abbey was the eminent hermit and theologian Gregory Palamas, who later became archbishop of Thessaloniki. Two times in the 16th century, pirates destroyed and plundered the abbey but it was rebuilt. In the 17th century the abbey fell into a decline but during the years of the Russian king Alexander Michaelovits, it received many contributions from Russia as well as from other Orthodox Christians which helped the abbeys' renovation.

In 1705, Gregory Melenikiou became monk in this abbey, giving life to the place. Half a century later Daniel from Thessaloniki was appointed commissioner of the abbey after he had won the approval by Patriarch Gerassimos and the 'Sacred Gathering'. After his appointment he transformed the abbey into a cenobetic one.

Suppertime.

Procession at Karyes.

Recess in the refectory of Vatopediou Monastery. ▶

During the Greek revolution of 1821, the Turks did great damage to the abbey. In the period 1850-1858, the new rows of cells were built. Except the main temple there are also eight chapels. The famous monk Anthony Petserski, founder of the famous Lavras abbey in Kiev, lived at the Esphigmenou abbey in the 11th century. Moreover, he applied the monastic customs of Greece in his country and he became the founder of the Russian monastic movement. Nowadays, he is honored as a saint.

The library which is situated over head, contains 320 hand-written codes, 75 of which are of parchment. Among them, one is erased and re-written. Several of the codes have excellent miniatures (like the code number 33 which has miniatures from the 11th century). The library also has 2.500 prints. The abbey's treasure collection, consists of the cross of Pulcheria, an excellent mosaic icon which dates back to the 13th century, sacerdotal vestments, portable icons, liturgical objects, sceptres, crosses, relics of saints, several valuable documents, an embroidered piece of Napoleon's tent in Egypt and others.

It is considered as one of the most strict cenobetic abbeys of Athos.

Life on Mount Athos.

Embroidered representation of Simonos Petra Monastery.

St George slaying the dragon and Xenofondos Monastery (copperplate engraving).

Stavronikita Monastery (copperplate engraving).

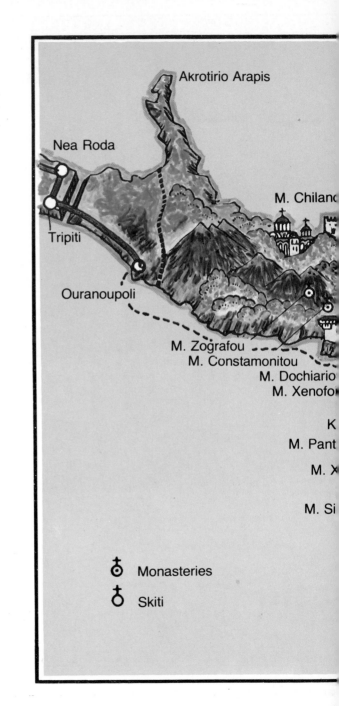

Akrotirio Arapis

Nea Roda

Tripiti

Ouranoupoli

M. Chiland

M. Zografou
M. Constamonitou
M. Dochiario
M. Xenofo

K
M. Pant

M. X

M. Si

Monasteries

Skiti

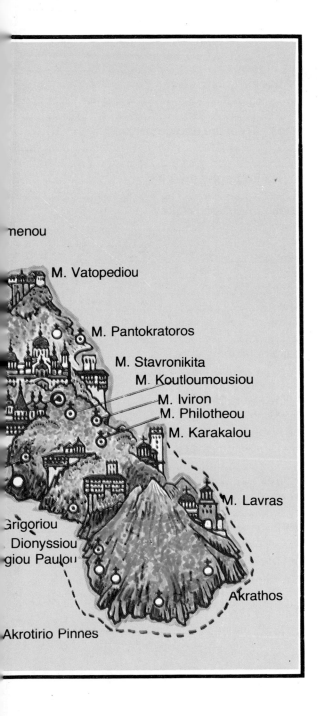

menou

M. Vatopediou

M. Pantokratoros

M. Stavronikita

M. Koutloumousiou

M. Iviron

M. Philotheou

M. Karakalou

M. Lavras

Grigoriou

Dionyssiou

giou Paulou

Akrathos

Akrotirio Pinnes

Contents